National Border Patrol Strategy

Office of Border Patrol

Contents

Executive Summary

In the wake of the terrorist attacks of September 11, 2001, the Border Patrol has experienced a tremendous change in its mission. With the formation of a new parent agency, U.S. Customs and Border Protection (CBP), the Border Patrol has as its priority mission preventing terrorists and terrorist weapons from entering the United States. The Border Patrol will continue to advance its traditional mission by preventing illegal aliens, smugglers, narcotics, and other contraband from entering the United States as these measures directly impact the safety and security of the United States.

To carry out its missions, the Border Patrol has a clear strategic goal: to establish and maintain operational control of the border of the United States. All of our efforts must be focused on this goal.

The Border Patrol's strategy consists of five main objectives:
- Establish substantial probability of apprehending terrorists and their weapons as they attempt to enter illegally between the ports of entry;
- Deter illegal entries through improved enforcement;
- Detect, apprehend, and deter smugglers of humans, drugs, and other contraband;
- Leverage "Smart Border" technology to multiply the effect of enforcement personnel; and
- Reduce crime in border communities and consequently improve quality of life and economic vitality of targeted areas.

To carry out these objectives, the Border Patrol will employ a highly centralized and strengthened

Photo: Horse Patrol Unit

organizational model with a direct chain of command from the Commissioner of CBP to the Chief of the Border Patrol to field locations. National guidance for planning and implementation will ensure that resources are focused in the highest risk areas and that the foundation for operational control over our Nation's border is established and maintained. Operational control is defined as the ability to detect, respond, and interdict border penetrations in areas deemed as high priority for threat potential or other national security objectives. Operational control may be limited to specific smuggling corridors or other geographically defined locations. This centralized structure will ensure accountability for the implementation and success of this Strategy.

This National Strategy will build on the successes of the previous 1994 "prevention through deterrence" Strategy. The Border Patrol will continue to acquire and deploy the proper balance of personnel, equipment, technology, and border infrastructure to achieve incremental and focused operational control of our Nation's borders. The Border Patrol will also strengthen and enhance its ability to rapidly deploy, both on a temporary and permanent basis, a highly motivated, well-trained workforce of agents to respond to potential terrorist and other national security threats. This response capability will include specialized teams within the Border Patrol who will provide a flexible and rapid response to potential terrorist incidents and other threats, both domestic and foreign.

Critical to the National Border Patrol Strategy will be the use of tactical, operational, and strategic intelligence to assess risk, target enforcement efforts, and drive operations. Intelligence collection and sharing efforts will be strengthened within the Department of Homeland Security and with outside agencies (federal, state, local). As part of its intelligence efforts, CBP Border Patrol will develop and deploy the next generation of border surveillance and sensoring platforms. These systems will maximize the Border Patrol's ability to detect, respond, and interdict cross-border intrusions and will increase the certainty of apprehension – especially in cases with a potential nexus to terrorism or which represent a threat to U.S. national security.

This Strategy provides the framework for the Border Patrol, as part of CBP, to plan and carry out its missions within the Department of Homeland Security. It provides the necessary goal, objectives, strategies, and measures for Border Patrol planning and operations and will be used as the basis for management decisions and resource deployment.

The National Border Patrol's Strategy directly supports CBP's 2006-2010 Strategic Plan. This strategy specifically addresses three of CBP's strategic goals, including:

- ***Preventing Terrorism***

  Detect and prevent terrorists and terrorist weapons, including weapons of mass effect, from entering the United States.

- ***Strengthening Our Control of the United States Borders***

  Strengthen national security between the ports of entry to prevent the illegal entry of terrorists, terrorist weapons, contraband, and illegal aliens into the United States.

- ***Protecting America and its Citizens***

  Contribute to a safer America by prohibiting the introduction of illicit contraband, including illegal drugs, and other harmful materials and organisms, into the United States.

Actions taken under this Strategy also complement work being done at the ports of entry by CBP officers and agricultural specialists, and draw on the support of many individuals throughout CBP, including intelligence analysts, information technology specialists, finance and logistics officers, and those with expertise in training and communication. Finally, this Strategy directly supports the strategic goals of the Department of Homeland Security to increase awareness, prevention, and protection against terrorism.

The Threat and Environment

The priority mission of CBP is to prevent terrorists and terrorist weapons from entering the United States. With the establishment of CBP, for the first time in our Nation's history, one agency within the U.S. government has responsibility for the security of our Nation's borders. CBP Border Patrol has primary responsibility for monitoring and responding to illicit border intrusions across thousands of miles of border between U.S. ports of entry.

Prior to the terrorist attacks of 9/11, the primary focus of the Border Patrol was on illegal aliens, alien smuggling, and narcotics interdiction. The Border Patrol arrests over one million illegal aliens annually, and routinely seizes over 1 million pounds of marijuana and 15 - 20 tons of cocaine every year. After 9/11, it was apparent that smugglers' methods, routes, and modes of transportation are potential vulnerabilities that can be exploited by terrorists and result in terrorist weapons illegally entering the United States. The Border Patrol's expertise in countering this threat is critical to ensuring the security of the United States.

Although the threat and strategic response vary across the Northern, Southern and Coastal Borders, the potential exists for a single individual or small group to cross the border undetected with biological or chemical weapons, weapons of mass effect, or other implements of terrorism. CBP's National Border Patrol Strategy has been developed with measures and initiatives designed to eliminate or mitigate this threat.

The Border Patrol will address a wide variety of threats and vulnerabilities by deploying an appropriate mix of personnel, equipment, technology, and border infrastructure. The differing threat locations outlined below result from the geographical diversity of the border and from other related

factors, such as differences in population centers, routes of ingress and egress from the border, economic stability of neighboring countries, and immigration patterns. These differences are wide-ranging and require the Border Patrol to maintain a high degree of flexibility in its approach to the border security mission.

Southern (U.S.–Mexico) Border:

The Southern Border with Mexico consists of approximately 2,000 miles of border, some of which is extremely inhospitable and harsh terrain. Hundreds of aliens die each year as a result of failed smuggling efforts while attempting to cross the Southern Border. Within these 2,000 miles of border, there are three primary smuggling corridors: South Texas corridor; West Texas/New Mexico corridor; and California/Arizona corridor. These corridors are largely dictated by transportation routes, geography, and population centers. More than ninety percent of the one million plus annual arrests that the Border Patrol makes occur along the U.S.-Mexico border within these smuggling corridors.

The Border Patrol has experienced success in gaining operational control of the border in some of the highest trafficked areas, such as San Diego, El Paso, and McAllen. However, many other areas along the southwest border are not yet under operational control, and the daily attempts to cross the border by thousands of illegal aliens from countries around the globe continue to present a threat to U.S. national security. Some would classify the majority of these aliens as "economic migrants." However, an ever-present threat exists from the potential for terrorists to employ the same smuggling and transportation networks, infrastructure, drop houses, and other support and then use these masses of illegal aliens as "cover" for a successful cross-border penetration.

The Border Patrol arrests hundreds of aliens each year from "special interest" countries. The

Photo: The U.S.–Mexico Border

State Department has determined that these countries present a potential terrorist threat to U.S. national security. Cross-border illegal penetrations by terrorists and those potentially smuggling terrorist weapons are not mutually exclusive from penetrations by illegal aliens, criminals, and narcotics traffickers.

Past experience has shown that a balanced mix of personnel, technology, and border infrastructure, such as roads, lights, fencing, and facilities, are critical to expanding control over the Southern Border. The Border Patrol will build on the successes won by the deployment of these resources on the Southern Border, and continue to expand state of the art sensoring technologies, intelligence, skills and training, and nationally driven deployment of personnel and material.

Northern (U.S.-Canada) Border:

The U.S.-Canada border consists of approximately 4,000 – 5,000 miles of border, some of which is water boundary and includes the Great Lakes area and surrounding waterways. Some of these waterways freeze during the winter and can easily be crossed on foot or by vehicle or snowmobile. Under this Strategy, the Border Patrol must also address issues inherent in locations along the Northern Border designated as reservation lands for Native American peoples, that allow more limited access on both the U.S. and Canadian sides of the border.

Further threats result from the fact that over ninety percent of Canada's population lives within one hundred miles of the U.S.-Canada border. Although the U.S. and Canada enjoy an extremely cooperative relationship, intelligence indicates that some individuals and organizations in Canada who reside near the border represent a potential threat to U.S. national security. The Northern Border also has well-organized smuggling operations, which can potentially support the movement of terrorists and their weapons.

The number of actual illegal border penetrations along the U.S.-Canada border is small in comparison to daily arrests along the U.S.-Mexico border. While resources have been significantly increased since 9/11 from approximately 350 agents to 1,000 agents, the Border Patrol's ability to detect, respond to, and interdict illegal cross-border penetrations along the U.S.-Canada border remains limited. Continued testing, acquisition, and deployment of sensing and monitoring platforms will be key to CBP Border Patrol's ability to effectively address the Northern Border threat situation.

To identify specific Northern Border threats, CBP Border Patrol has strengthened its partnerships with Canadian law enforcement and intelligence officials, and with officials from other federal, state, local, and tribal organizations by leveraging information and increasing communication and cooperation. The Integrated Border Enforcement, Maritime, and Intelligence Teams (IBET/IMET/ IBIT) are examples of this effort, which the Border Patrol will continue to strengthen under this Strategy.

Coastal (Caribbean) Borders:

In the U.S. Coastal areas, the Border Patrol works with a variety of law enforcement agencies, such as the U.S. Coast Guard, to address the threat of potential mass migrations, maritime smuggling, and crewman control. While the number of illegal entrants migrating through Coastal areas is currently lower than on the land borders, the threat faced by the Border Patrol is increased by local government corruption and inadequate tracking systems which fail to monitor those who transit those countries.

The proximity of these nations to the United States coastline requires that all CBP components remain vigilant and promote a common operational picture. Therefore, investing in air and maritime assets, continuing partnerships with other DHS components, and leveraging available assets operating in this environment are critical to ensuring that CBP has flexible response capabilities to address the threat in Coastal sectors.

National Objectives

This National Strategy identifies the objectives, tools, and initiatives the Border Patrol needs to meet its priority goal: to establish and maintain operational control over our Nation's borders. The objectives outlined below directly support CBP's mission "to control U.S. borders to prevent entry into the United States of terrorists and terrorist weapons." The focus on these strategic Border Patrol objectives is critical and must be at the forefront of planning throughout the CBP organization.

Five overarching objectives were developed to guide the Border Patrol in the planning and implementation of this National Strategy. These objectives will serve as the focus for planning and implementation, both nationally and at the sector and station levels.

Border Patrol Honor Guard

Objective 1

Establish substantial probability of apprehending terrorists and their weapons as they attempt to illegally enter the United States between the ports of entry

This objective directly supports the priority mission of the Border Patrol, which is detecting and preventing terrorists and terrorist weapons from entering the country between official ports of entry. The Border Patrol has a number of actions it will take to meet this objective. Among these initiatives are enhancement of partnerships with other federal, state, local, and tribal law enforcement agencies. In addition, the Border Patrol will pursue the strategic deployment of monitoring and sensoring platforms to increase the ability to detect, respond to, and interdict cross-border incursions. This will ensure that the Border Patrol responds to changes in criminal tactics in a comprehensive fashion, leaving minimal weaknesses to be exploited by terrorists or other criminals. It will also ensure that law enforcement officers can adjust to changes brought about by increased enforcement in adjoining sectors, ports of entry, or other vulnerable areas.

Continued testing, acquisition, and deployment of technologies and initiatives to identify terrorists and their weapons will be critical. Examples include the Integrated Automated Fingerprint Identification System (IAFIS), and radiation detection and monitoring equipment at Border Patrol checkpoints and other strategic locations. These technologies will be complemented by rapid response teams such as the Border Patrol Tactical Team (BORTAC), the Border Patrol Search, Trauma, and Rescue Team (BORSTAR), Special Response Teams (SRT), and bomb and alien detection canines.

The Border Patrol will increase the use of targeting information from the National Targeting Center and other data and intelligence sources to identify potential terrorists. In coordination with CBP's Office of Anti-Terrorism, the Border Patrol will also increase participation in Joint Terrorism Task Force units where operationally feasible. In addition, the Border Patrol will rely on CBP's overseas assets in key locations, such as Canada and Mexico City, for information and operational support.

Objective 2

Deter illegal entries through improved enforcement

The Border Patrol's 1994 Strategy was based on a philosophy of "prevention through deterrence." This direction has proven effective in key high-traffic corridors along the southwest border, near San Diego, El Paso, McAllen, and most recently, Tucson. The control resulting from this Strategy is even more important in the post–9/11 environment as any illegal entry could be a terrorist.

To control the border, the 1994 Strategy relied on the strategic deployment of a mix of personnel, equipment, technology, and border infrastructure, including all-weather roads, lights, and fencing. In addition to deploying these assets along the immediate border, the Border Patrol used checkpoint operations to further control potential routes of egress, and these have been critical to the success of border enforcement operations.

Photo: All Terrain Vehicle Unit

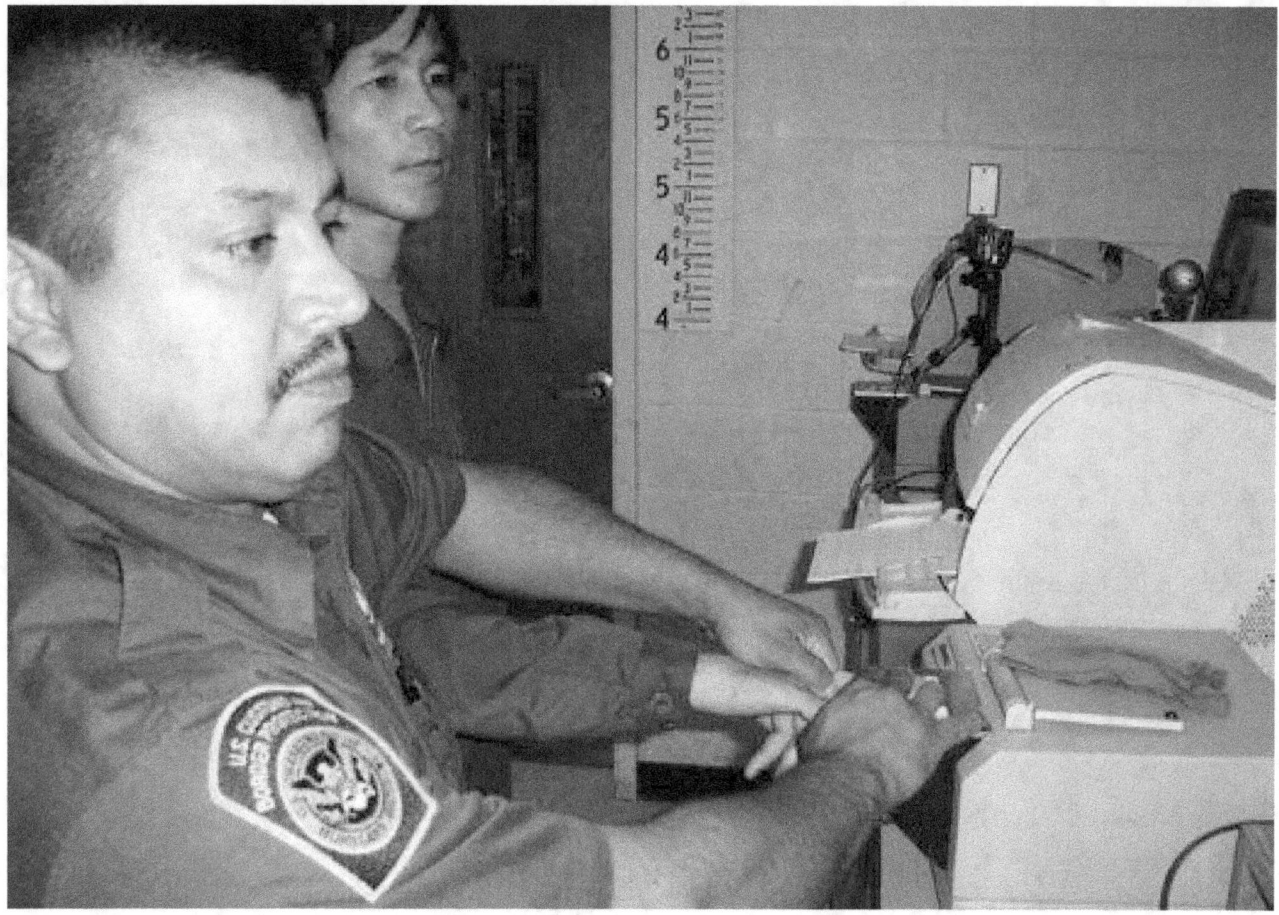

Past success has demonstrated that effective deployment of the proper mix of assets increases the "certainty of apprehension" of those intending to illegally cross our borders. Certainty of apprehension, along with a vigorous prosecution strategy for recidivists and smugglers, has established a deterrent effect in targeted locations. This strategic approach to border control has set the foundation for establishing focused operational control for other areas along our Nation's borders, especially in high-traffic/high-threat areas where illegal border-crossing and smuggling is prevalent.

CBP must continue similar strategies to gain, maintain, and expand operational control to other priority corridors. These priority areas will be defined by threat analysis to guide resource deployment and decision-making. Maintaining and expanding a strong enforcement posture along U.S. borders, including sufficient flexibility to address dynamic enforcement challenges, is critical to bringing operational control to our borders. Coordination with the Office of Field Operations and potential impact on ports of entry will be included in planning and analysis, as will partnership with the Offices of Anti-Terrorism and Intelligence.

Objective 3

Apprehend and deter smugglers of humans, drugs, and other contraband

The Border Patrol also maintains its traditional mission of preventing the entry and smuggling of illegal aliens, narcotics, and other contraband from entering the United States between official ports of entry. Drug and alien smuggling has become an increasingly sophisticated and complex criminal enterprise. The Border Patrol will continue to deploy its resources in order to meet geographic and threat requirements to detect, interdict, and respond to alien smugglers, smugglers of illicit narcotics, and other contraband. The ability to collect, share, and process intelligence, data, and other information will be important to the detection, identification, and prosecution of criminal aliens, smugglers, and their networks. The Border Patrol and the Office of Information Technology must continue to test, acquire, and deploy technology to assist agents to detect and identify alien smugglers, criminals, and narcotics traffickers. Further partnership with

Photo: Border Patrol agent using IDENT/IAFIS to identify and document an alien 9

the National Targeting Center, the development and use of tactical and strategic intelligence, and the expansion of IAFIS is also important to this objective.

The Border Patrol, in coordination with Immigration and Customs Enforcement (ICE), will continue to expand its ability to target cross-border smuggling operations, consistent with agreed upon roles and responsibilities. The Border Patrol's continued participation and expansion in task force operations will also be a component of achieving this objective when operationally feasible and necessary.

Objective 4

Leverage "Smart Border" technology to multiply the effect of enforcement personnel

The Border Patrol currently uses a mix of agents, information, and technology to control the border. The Border Patrol's ability to establish situational awareness, monitor, detect, respond to, and identify potential terrorists, instruments of terrorism, and criminals relies heavily on interdiction and deterrence-based technology. Having the necessary technology to support the Border Patrol priority and traditional missions cannot be overstated. In the future, there must be continued assessment, development, and deployment of the appropriate mix of personnel, technology, and information to gain, maintain, and expand coverage of the border and ensure that resources are deployed in a cost-effective, efficient fashion.

Technology which enhances operational awareness and effectiveness includes camera systems for day/night/infrared work, biometric systems such as IDENT/IAFIS, processing systems like ENFORCE, sensoring platforms, large-scale gamma X-rays, and aerial platforms, and other systems. Technologies requiring modernization include wireless and tactical communications and computer processing capabilities.

Coordination between Border Patrol and inspectional personnel at the ports of entry ensures the most efficient use of trained personnel and technology. In the future, the Border Patrol will take advantage of the targeting and selectivity tools made available in the Automated Commercial Environment (ACE) and the

Photo: Border Patrol agent monitoring Remote Video Surveillance cameras

National Targeting Center. The continued testing, evaluation, acquisition, and deployment of appropriate border enforcement technologies will be pursued vigorously so that the maximum force-multiplier effect is achieved in support of both the priority and traditional missions.

Objective 5

Reduce crime in border communities and consequently improve the quality of life and economic vitality of regions

Past successes in border enforcement operations have demonstrated that a border under operational control directly correlates to reduced crime associated as high levels of illegal border incursions significantly impact border communities. The overall quality of life of border residents, economic expansion, and environmental protection significantly improves in areas where the Border Patrol's Strategy has been successfully implemented. The Border Patrol will continue to deploy resources and conduct public outreach in areas deemed high-threat or high-priority to improve the overall quality of life, reduce social service costs, and decrease crime in border areas.

By maintaining an active presence in border communities, Border Patrol agents provide a deterrent to active smuggling, partner with local residents to identify illegal activity, and support cooperative local law enforcement efforts in both urban and remote areas of the country. The Border Patrol will also continue to expand and strengthen its current Border Safety Initiative to enhance the safety of migrants and border residents.

Tactics and Technology

The following represents the tactical and technological approaches, under the direction of the CBP Commissioner and Chief of the Border Patrol, that the Border Patrol will pursue in addressing this Strategy's objectives: a more flexible, well-trained, nationally-directed Border Patrol; specialized teams and rapid-response capabilities; intelligence-driven operations; and infrastructure, facility, and technology support.

Approach 1

A more flexible, well-trained, nationally-directed Border Patrol

The Border Patrol will use a highly centralized organizational model with a direct chain of command from the CBP Commissioner, to the Chief of the Border Patrol, to the Sector Chief Patrol Agents. This national command structure will facilitate national determinations on threat and resource priorities and will allow for the rapid deployment of Border Patrol assets, both on a short-term, temporary basis, as well as on long-term or permanent operations. This nationally directed mobility, with supporting national policies, will allow the Border Patrol to rapidly respond to emerging threats and hot spots along the border in a proactive prevention and response capacity. This type of flexibility is critical to address the present terrorist threat.

Anti-terrorism training is critical to ensuring that Border Patrol agents are fully prepared to address the terrorism threat. In conjunction with the Office of Training and Development, the Border Patrol will continually assess its anti-terrorism training requirements to ensure that agents, supervisors, and managers have the necessary multi-disciplinary training to effectively

Border Patrol agents patrol the waters of the Rio Grande River

carry out the Border Patrol's priority anti-terrorism mission. The Office of Training and Development will work with the Border Patrol to ensure this training is developed and delivered in the most effective and operationally efficient manner, using methods such as computer-based modules, mobile training teams, train-the-trainer instruction, classroom and Academy training.

The Border Patrol will continue to deploy assets to interior U.S. locations where there is a direct nexus to border control operations, such as at transportation hubs, airports, and bus stations to confront routes of egress for terrorists, smugglers, and illegal aliens, and to support ICE-led interior efforts when appropriately coordinated and approved at the national level.

Approach 2

Specialized teams and rapid-response capabilities

CBP will expand the training and response capabilities of the Border Patrol's specialized BORTAC, BOR-STAR, and Special Response teams to support domestic and international intelligence-driven and anti-terrorism efforts as well as other special operations. These teams will assist in terrorism prevention through planning, training, and tactical deployment. As a highly mobile, rapid-response tool, they will significantly increase CBP's ability to respond operationally to specific terrorist threats and incidents, as well as to support the traditional Border Patrol mission.

Photo: BORSTAR team removes an injured person from the southwest desert

Approach 3

Intelligence-driven operations

The Border Patrol will expand the use of national security and terrorist-related intelligence and targeting information to improve intelligence-driven operations. This will enable the Border Patrol to deploy its resources effectively to target areas of greatest risk. These operations will be coordinated with the Office of Field Operations to ensure maximum effectiveness at and between the ports of entry. In order to support tactical and strategic operations, the Border Patrol will enhance its own organic intelligence program by coordinating with CBP's Office of Intelligence. In addition, the Border Patrol will leverage the intelligence capabilities of the Offices of Intelligence, Field Operations, and Anti-Terrorism to increase threat assessment, targeting efforts, operational planning, and communication to support its anti-terrorism and traditional missions.

Approach 4

Infrastructure, facility, and technology support

Integrating increased numbers of agents and new technology into the Border Patrol's enforcement activities has strained resources previously dedicated to infrastructure, facility, and technology support. To ensure the objectives of this Strategy are not negatively impacted by a degradation of its infrastructure, the Border Patrol will continue to assess and address critical needs for this support, which include new construction; the preservation of buildings, technology, vehicles, and fences; and the deployment and maintenance of new technologies, ranging from remote cameras to computer and intelligence systems. This support is critical to ensuring that the investment made in new agents and new technology maintains its effectiveness in the face of shifting patterns of border threat and changing criminal tactics.

Photo: Unmanned Aerial Vehicle (UAV) takes a test flight over the Arizona desert

Strategies to Address Areas of Threat

Southern Border

Strategic Focus:

- Achieve proper balance between personnel, equipment, technology, and border infrastructure;

- Gain, maintain, and expand control of borders based on threat and priority; and

- Enhance rapid response capabilities.

Anti-terrorism concerns result in part from the risk of terrorists becoming lost in the massive flow of illegal immigration along the Southern Border and the potential use of well-established smuggling networks. The strategic approach on the Southern Border is to leverage the success of the 1994 Border Patrol Strategy, which focused on deployment of the proper balance of personnel, equipment, technology, border infrastructure, and the establishment of a "prevention through deterrence" posture. The continued expansion of this Strategy will deter smuggling and illegal entries by reducing smugglers' ability to use existing infrastructure to facilitate their operations. The Border Patrol will also strengthen and expand partnerships with other law enforcement agencies to increase the overall enforcement density along our country's borders.

To carry out this approach on the Southern Border, CBP Border Patrol will:
- Deter or deny access to urban areas, infrastructure, transportation, and routes of egress to smuggling organizations through checkpoints, intelligence-driven special operations, and targeted patrols;
- Expand control through increased and more mobile personnel and improved air and ground support;
- Increase rapid response capabilities;
- Continue and expand the appropriate mix of improved infrastructure and technology;
  - Sensing systems, Remote Video Surveillance and Sensing (RVSS) cameras, air support, and Unmanned Aerial Vehicles (UAVs)
  - Radiation detection equipment
  - Improved communication infrastructure (Land Mobile Radio, cellular coverage, satellite communication capabilities)
  - Remote access to national law enforcement databases through the use of mobile computing solutions

- - Mobile alien processing capabilities to support field enforcement activities
- - Checkpoints and high-intensity enforcement zones
- - Roads, lights, fencing, and vehicle barriers
- • Expand cooperation with other agencies; and
- • Continue deterrence efforts.

The primary challenges will be improved detection and surveillance capabilities to augment and support existing agent resources and to address developing and dynamic threats and vulnerabilities, which will require significant fiscal investment. Other challenges include increasing cooperation with Mexico on policies to improve safety and slow migration.

Photo: Border Patrol agents on the southwest border

Strategies to Address Areas of Threat

Northern Border

Strategic Focus:

- Balance intelligence use, other agency liaison efforts, technology, and equipment use, and personnel;
- Identify threat areas and resource requirements to mitigate and defeat threats;
- Acquire communications and data infrastructure to support detection and response;
- Expand detection technologies and sensing platforms; and
- Improve mobility and rapid response capability.

The Northern Border presents unique challenges. The Border Patrol recognizes that the geographic distinctions along the Northern Border yield a much greater vulnerability for terrorist border-crossing attempts. The challenges and expanses along the Northern Border highlight the need for improved detection and response capabilities. Response levels have been strengthened by an increase in agents along the Northern Border since the 9/11 terrorist attacks. These agents will require more detection and communication technologies since the ratio of agent to miles of terrain will remain high. An improved communication and data infrastructure will be required to support sensor detection, identification, and response to terrorists and their weapons. Improved technologies would include sensors and cameras appropriate to the terrain and weather; new platforms such as UAVs, lighter-than-air ships or satellites to improve detection effectiveness, and signal intercept devices. Enhanced response will also be facilitated through the acquisition of additional aviation assets capable of light observation, medium lift, or fixed-wing flight.

The creation of Border Patrol-led joint task forces with state, local, and tribal law enforcement and the expansion of the Canadian IBET initiatives will also support prevention and response efforts. Intelligence with predictive value will allow the Border Patrol to identify and respond to terrorism threats as a matter of national priority.

To carry out this approach on the Northern Border, CBP Border Patrol will:
- Ensure sufficient mobile workforce levels;
- Expand communications and data infrastructure to support sensing and response capability;
- Develop and expand sensing/camera/UAV technology;
- Acquire and use additional air assets;
- Use checkpoints and other deterrents;

- Create BP-led joint task forces with state/local/tribal law enforcement;
- Expand upon existing IBET initiatives; and
- Improve the dissemination of actionable intelligence.

Challenges include obtaining sufficient funding for the technology infrastructure; fielding adequate numbers of sensing systems, platforms, and mobility assets, and improving the transportation and building infrastructure for Border Patrol operations on the Northern Border.

Photo: Border Patrol agent preparing to patrol the waterways near Buffalo, NY in an OH–6 helicopter

Strategies to Address Areas of Threat

Coastal Border

Strategic Focus:

- Enhance and improve cooperative law enforcement efforts;
- Establish and employ a common operational picture; and
- Expand and enhance interagency planning and operations.

The Coastal Border is disparate in terms of threat and response capabilities. In general, there is not daily mass migration, although the threat of migration emergencies from unstable geopolitical situations can be very high. The Coastal Border also has a higher number of law enforcement agencies that actively coordinate daily operations and has more limited platform requirements for detection. In addition, the mode of transportation for enforcement and illegal entry or smuggling is unique to this environment, as are the safety considerations for waterborne enforcement.

The core concepts for the Coastal Border are similar to those for the Southern and Northern Borders – gain, maintain, and expand shallow and deep-water control in the areas of responsibility in support of the priority anti-terrorism mission. A key strategy to accomplishing this mission is partnership and integration with other law enforcement agency efforts. Due to the size of the geographic area that must be policed and the uniqueness of the environment, the attainment of our mission in this area requires clear, coordinated, federal, state, and local law enforcement activities. Interagency planning and operations will be expanded to provide a well-coordinated response to Coastal threats. The Border Patrol will also work with the U.S. Coast Guard and CBP personnel in the ports of entry to detect and apprehend absconding maritime crewmen.

To carry out this approach on the Coastal Border, CBP Border Patrol will:
- Right-size the maritime fleet;
- Prepare for incidence of mass migration; and
- Conduct threat analysis of future Coastal vulnerabilities.

Challenges for CBP in the pursuit of these strategic initiatives include acquisition of funding for Coastal environment sensing systems, platforms, and maritime fleet assets, and increasing cooperation and collaboration with other law enforcement entities.

Strategic Outcome Measures

CBP views its performance measurement environment as dynamic. Through its Strategic Plan and other planning and budget documents, CBP strives to maintain the purpose of the Government Performance and Results Act; improving program efficiency and effectiveness, which includes maintaining a results-oriented focus that clearly describes program goals and objectives. Developing an integrated planning methodology that is supported by meaningful performance measures is a key component in demonstrating business results.

It is often difficult to measure quantitatively how well a law enforcement organization is meeting its challenges. CBP is no exception. Measuring program effectiveness in law enforcement is complex. Although traditional workload measures are a valuable indicator of the challenges CBP Border Patrol faces, they do not always reflect the success or failure of the agency's efforts. The direct impact being made on unlawful activity is often unknown. Because of these and other unknown variables, the traditional economics and methodologies of measuring performance can be particularly challenging.

Although limitations exist, CBP continues to refine its existing measures as well as propose new ones. To mitigate this challenge, CBP has adopted a mix of qualitative and quantitative measures. Workload statistics augment these measures because CBP views its workload as preventing windows of opportunity for potential smuggling.

Since September 11, 2001, CBP has focused its activities on homeland security and protecting the American public from acts of terrorism. As part of the post-September 11 analysis, CBP determined that its effectiveness to secure the U.S. border should continue to be measured in both

qualitative and quantitative terms. As a result, CBP is developing a new list of potential measures which will help gauge success in these areas, as well as the success of other increased enforcement and facilitation efforts.

The new measures under development reflect the new programs and the priority efforts used in combating terrorism outlined in the National Border Patrol Strategy. The following examples show the types of metrics that CBP is considering for use in assessing the agency's effectiveness at combating terrorism between the ports of entry:

- Expand Border Patrol Operational Planning Model to six high-priority and high-threat sectors beyond the original implementation in the Tucson Sector for FY 2005;
- Create a chronology of measurable and anecdotal terrorism-related enforcement successes;
- Increase operational area-specific apprehensions through more targeted enforcement;
- Increase and improve testing, acquisition, and deployment of technologies and initiatives to identify terrorists and their weapons;
- Reduce overall recidivism, based on a strong law enforcement posture;
- Identify and deny smuggling corridors as measured by the number of smuggling route-deflections;
- Increase and improve deployment of Smart Border technology; and
- Improve quality-of-life in Border communities as measured by indicators such as lower crime rates and reduced costs to taxpayers for cross-border activity related burdens.

There is no one way to measure the effectiveness of CBP efforts to combat terrorism. However, the performance metrics currently being considered by CBP will measure how various initiatives will assist in securing the border between the ports of entry and complement other national CBP initiatives.

Photo: Border Patrol honor guard holds flag during the CBP Annual Law Enforcement Memorial Ceremony   21